P9-CQW-466

OPTICAL ILLUSIONS

LAURENCE B. WHITE, JR.,
AND RAY BROEKEL

OPTICAL ILLUSIONS

FRANKLIN WATTS
NEW YORK | LONDON | TORONTO | SYDNEY | 1986
A FIRST BOOK

DIAGRAMS BY ANNE CANEVARI GREEN

Photographs courtesy of:
George and Judy Manna/Photo Researchers: p. 10;
Victor Engelbert/Photo Researchers: p. 72;
Robert C. Hermes from National Audubon Society/
Photo Researchers: p. 73.

The original Orville Meyer card is included on
page 68 with his permission.

Library of Congress Cataloging-in-Publication Data

White, Laurence B.
Optical illusions.

(A First book)
Bibliography: p.
Includes index.
Summary: Explains how optical illusions trick the
eye and fool perception and provides examples and
instructions for readers to make their own.
1. Optical illusions—Juvenile literature.
(1. Optical illusions) I. Broekel, Ray. II. Green,
Anne Canevari, ill. III. Title.
QP495.W48 1986   152.1'48   86-10986
ISBN 0-531-10220-3

CONTENTS

OTHER BOOKS BY
LAURENCE B. WHITE, JR.
AND RAY BROEKEL

Easy Magic for Beginners
The Trick Book
The Surprise Book
Abbra-ca-Dazzle
Hocus Pocus

TO THE BARE BEARS
OF THE WORLD

OPTICAL
ILLUSIONS

Figure 1

1

SEEING
IS
DECEIVING

A picture is worth a thousand words!

It's a common expression, and it certainly sounds like a true one. To prove it, try this right now: Describe, using *words only* (no fair using your hands to help), a spiral staircase. Just pretend you have a friend who has never seen one.

It's extremely hard. How many words did you use? Now, look at the picture of a spiral staircase in Figure 1.

How many words would you have saved if you could have shown your friend this picture? Perhaps not a thousand, but certainly hundreds. This old expression would seem to be absolutely correct. However, this book is about things that are not always as they seem, so you might save a thousand words with the spiral staircase picture—but not with all pictures. Some pictures can't be trusted! (Figure 2 on page 12 is one to watch out for.)

Unless you *see* things differently from most people, this picture will make no sense at first. In fact, you will probably have to read the *words* that follow, plus use your brain, to know just what you are seeing, because this picture is an *optical illusion*. Some optical illusions are pictures that need "a thousand words" to understand!

Begin your investigation into the amazing world of optical illusions by first looking at the two words, optical and illusion.

Optical tells you it has to do with eyes and seeing. An *illusion* is something that appears in some way different than it actually is. For example, a magician's trick is an illusion. A person is not really sawed in half, it only appears that way! It is the "illusion" part of "optical illusions" that makes them such fun to observe. The science of *why* they work makes them even more fun to study.

Figure 2

The optical illusion in Figure 2 confuses us because we are used to seeing bold, dark, filled-in letters making words. That's the way we have seen letters printed all our lives.

An artist calls the space around an object *negative space* and almost always the negative space around letters on a page is lighter than (sometimes darker, but always in contrast with) the letters so they can be easily read. This is the way the letters and words appear in this book in the sentence you are reading right now. If the publishers made both the letters and the negative space around them the same, the book would be an optical illusion! That is simply not the way our eyes and brain expect to see printed words!

Figure 2 (perhaps you've seen it by now?) is a picture of the *word* PICTURE. To see it you have to look at the spaces *between* the letters. Aren't you glad the publishers did not print all of the words in this book this way?

BRAIN WORK

Negative space is only one trick for creating, and under-standing, optical illusions. Let's experiment with another common expression: *seeing is believing.*

There's certainly something wrong with the picture frame in Figure 3. Perhaps you are saying, "I see it, but I don't believe it? What's fooling me here?" It's your *brain*!

To begin to understand the science of optical illusions, always remember one important fact: To see anything requires more than just your eyes. If you were reading this book at night and the lights suddenly went out, could you see? Of course not. Besides your eyes, light is necessary for sight. You also need a brain to let you understand what you are seeing. Your eyes and your brain work together, with

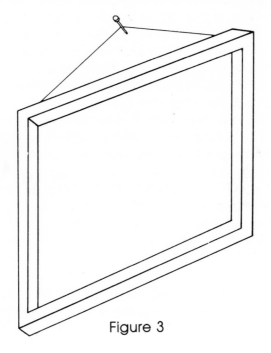

Figure 3

light, to enable you to see. If any one of these three is missing, you cannot see. And if any one of them is "confused," an optical illusion is the result.

Figure 3 confused your brain, because it was not the way your brain has learned to expect to see a picture frame. The "frame" confuses your brain. It does not confuse your eye one little bit. Your eye sees exactly what it is, some black lines drawn on a flat page.

Your eye sees only lines, but your *brain* takes right over and tries to make sense out of the drawing. Your brain tries to make it into something it has seen before—a picture frame, perhaps? But when your brain begins to try, it knows that picture frames aren't built like this. In fact, your brain knows that picture frames can't be built like this. So your brain is puzzled, confused, bewildered and you simply solve the whole thing by saying, "Boy, is that neat! It's an optical illusion."

Try this. Show a friend the "frame" picture but cover the left side with your palm. Your friend can see only the right side, which appears normal. Then slide your hand over to cover the right side so your friend sees only the left side. The left side appears normal too.

Now slide your hand back and forth so your friend sees each side for a moment, one following the other, several times. At first the picture, seen half at a time, will seem quite ordinary. Then, slowly, your friend will discover that the two sides don't seem to belong together. Explain that perhaps when he or she sees both sides it should all be clear, then take your hand away.

EYE WORK

Eyes, as you will discover in a chapter to come, are like cameras that take exceptionally fine and detailed pictures. It is

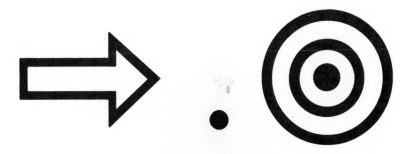

Figure 4

extremely difficult to create optical illusions that fool eyes. But knowing some facts about our eyes allows us to use these facts to confuse them. Take the fact that you have two eyes.

The arrow and target printed in Figure 4 cannot move. Your eyes are showing your brain that fact right now. But start to move the book closer to your eyes. Move the book up toward your eyes until your nose touches the dot between the arrow and the target. You will "shoot" the arrow right at the target! This works because when the page is close to your face, one eye sees only the arrow while the other eye sees only the target. Your brain must put the two pictures together.

You can have an "archery contest" using this optical illusion. Rotate the book slightly to the right or left and shoot the arrow again. This time you will *miss* the target. Depending on which way you turn the book you will shoot either too high or too low. Try again, rotating it in the other direction. With a few moments' practice you can shoot the arrow anywhere you wish.

LIGHT WORK

Light also fools us occasionally. Have you ever dropped something in the water when you were swimming and when you reached for it you discovered it was not quite where it appeared to be? Water distorts and bends light rays passing through it so the image (made up of light rays) may appear in a place different than the actual object. Let's make a coin vanish by causing its image to bend away from our eyes (Figure 5).

Place a coin on the table and set a glass on top. Look at the coin through the sides of the glass. It is easily seen. Now fill the glass with water and place a saucer on top. No matter where you look now, the coin is impossible to see! The light rays forming its image have been bent to the top, under the saucer!

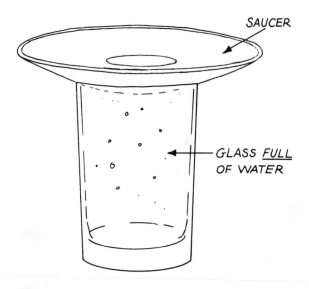

SAUCER

GLASS _FULL_ OF WATER

Figure 5

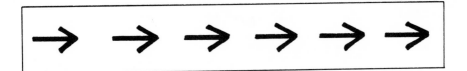

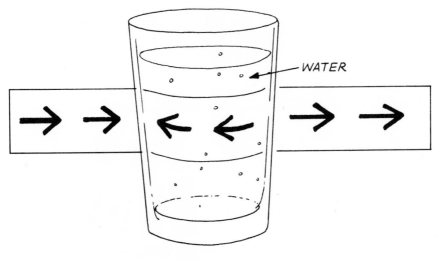

WATER

Figure 6

Lift the saucer off and look straight down into the water and you will see the coin easily. Light, bending, created this optical illusion of a coin vanishing.

Bending light can create still other illusions. Draw a line of small arrows on a strip of paper as shown in Figure 6. Slide the strip across behind the glassful of water (it will not work without water in the glass) and you will discover that the arrows on either side face one way but the arrows seen through the water have magically (actually, optically) reversed direction. As you slide the strip back and forth the arrows will twist back and forth in different directions.

LOOK IN
A
MIRROR

TURN
BOOK
UPSIDE
DOWN

KID—
DO HIDE
BOX & BIKE

Figure 7

You have begun to "look" at optical illusions a bit differently. Everyone looks at them for fun. You have started to learn some of the science of why they work. And you now know that optical illusions may result from a "mistake" of light, eye, or brain. Let's close this chapter, as we began it, with a mystery.

LIGHT, EYE, OR BRAIN WORK?

Hold this book upside down facing into a mirror. Look at the reflections of the three boxes in Figure 7. Each does something different.

In the first box all of the words are upside down and backward. In the second box one word, *book*, reads right side up. The other words are upside down and backward. In the third box, all of the words are right side up!

Why? When you first see it happen it seems impossible, but there is an answer. Do the words fool our brain, or do the light images coming from the mirror, or do mirrors confuse our eyes? It has to be one of these. Perhaps you will discover the answer in one of the chapters that follow.

2

GUESS
WHAT?

In the make-believe world of optical illusion there lived two sisters, Optic Ann and Fool U. Sue. People always said how alike they were, except for their mouths. In fact, it was by their mouths that people told them apart. Ann's mouth appeared sad and small, while Sue's mouth always wore a broad grin. You can see the sisters' mouths in Figure 8.

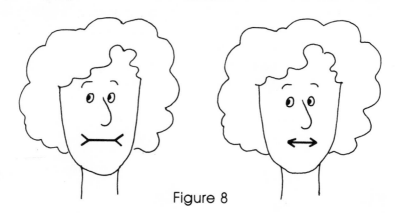

Figure 8

How wrong people were! As you have probably guessed, both sisters' mouths were exactly the same length (measure them yourself). It was only the creases at the edges of their mouths that created this optical illusion.

People who *guess* the length of Ann and Sue's mouths are fooled by an old, well-known optical illusion called the Muller-Leyer angle illusion. The moral of this make-believe story is: never completely trust your eyes and brain. Don't *guess* or an optical illusion might "get" you.

Why does the Muller-Leyer angle illusion work? Why do those tiny angles at the ends of each mouth line make such a difference? Some scientists think it is because we relate them to real things in our world. Perhaps we see them as a corner of a wall or a building, as shown in Figure 9.

In the drawing on the left, the lines are fading "far away", like an object at a distance. Your brain has learned that distant objects appear *smaller*. The lines in the figure on the right seem to be coming toward you. Your brain has learned that close objects appear *larger*.

Of course, this is just one explanation. Perhaps one day a better one will be found.

Figure 9

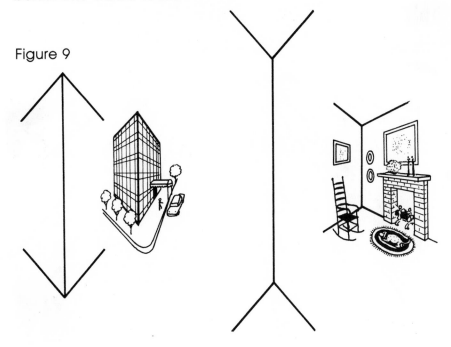

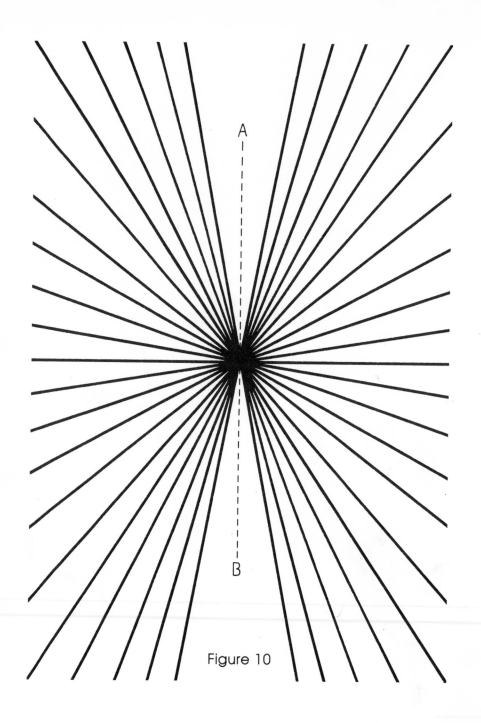

Figure 10

EYES FOLLOW LINES

People familiar with optical illusions are extremely careful never to make guesses when lines that radiate (move outward) or converge (move inward) are involved. A man hanging wallpaper with stripes always uses his ruler and level, never his eye, to be sure his stripes stay straight!

Experiment for yourself. Find a pencil that is perfectly straight and the same diameter all along its length. As you study this pencil with your eye and brain you will say it is perfectly straight and the same diameter all along its length. But what would you say if some carefully drawn lines were behind the pencil?

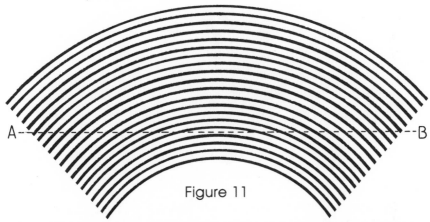

Figure 11

Lay your pencil across the diagrams in Figures 10 and 11, putting one end at A and the other end at B. One look at the center of the pencil and you will discover it no longer appears the same diameter all along its length on the first drawing or perfectly straight when laying on the second drawing. If the pencil had been lying on either of these diagrams when you first went to reach for it you would probably not have selected it. Your guess would have been that it was too fat or too crooked. You would have been wrong.

DISTANCE IS DIFFICULT

One of the hardest "guesses" you can ask your brain to make is judging distance, yet we do it all the time. How well can you guess distance? Here's a test you can take right now.

You'll need a handful of coins. They can be any denomination but must all be the same kind. Set two of them on a table a short distance (about the length of a pencil) apart. Study the space between the two, and guess how many coins will fit into that space. See Figure 12.

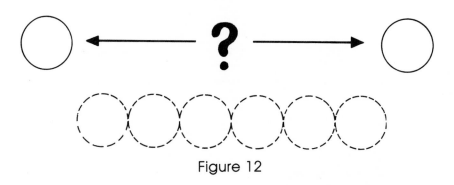

Figure 12

It's easy to check your guess: simply put actual coins in between them and see. You probably will find you guessed too many. Most people do. The amazing thing is that if you try the experiment several more times, changing the distances between the two starting coins each time, you will be wrong time and time again. However, your guesses will improve.

Next try it this way. Set one coin on the table and try to put the other coin exactly five coin lengths away from it. Is that any easier? If not, don't be discouraged: you are as normal as everyone else in the world. People have great difficulty guessing distance and space, and one reason is because optical illusions often get in the way.

Greater distances, outdoors for example, are even harder to estimate. Our brains have learned many facts that sometimes help us and sometimes hinder us. Let's look at three of these facts and experiment with them.

FAR AND NEAR "CLUES"

Fact number one: An object closer to you appears lighter in color than an object further away.

Look outdoors and you can see the truth of this fact. Nearby buildings or trees do appear lighter than similar objects in the distance. Distant objects tend to look gray and fuzzy. In Figure 13, however, *neither* tree is closer to you, since they both are printed side by side on a flat page. But because your brain "knows" that dark things are usually further away, you probably said the light-colored tree looked closer.

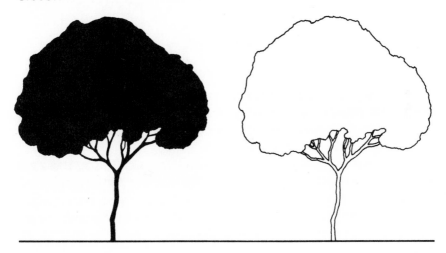

Figure 13

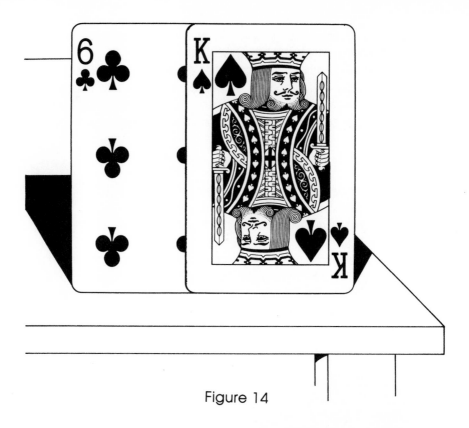

Figure 14

Fact number two: Closer objects overlap distant objects. Figure 14 shows two playing cards standing on edge on a table. If these were real cards on a real table, which one would be closer to your eye?

Because the king overlaps the six, you would say the king is closer, and ordinarily you would be correct. But if you have two old playing cards (any values will work) you can create an illusion so that your friends will guess wrong. You will need a shoebox without the cover, two cards, tape, and scissors. See Figure 15.

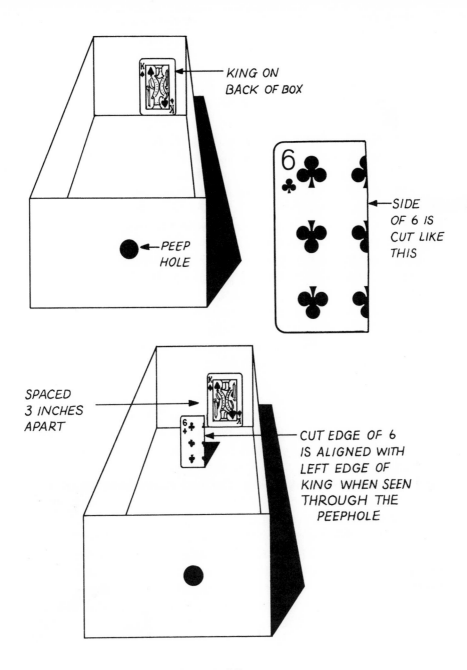

KING ON
BACK OF BOX

PEEP
HOLE

SIDE
OF 6 IS
CUT LIKE
THIS

SPACED
3 INCHES
APART

CUT EDGE OF 6
IS ALIGNED WITH
LEFT EDGE OF
KING WHEN SEEN
THROUGH THE
PEEPHOLE

Figure 15

Punch a peep hole through one end of the box. (This illusion must be viewed using only one eye looking in exactly the right place.) Tape one card to the inside of the other end of the box, slightly to one side of the center, its face toward the peephole.

Prepare the other card by cutting about one-third of it off lengthwise. Position it carefully inside the box. Hold it upright inside the box, face toward the peephole, about three or four inches away from the card taped to the end.

Look in the peephole and move the prepared card so that the cut edge lines up exactly with the edge of the card on the rear flap. When the card is positioned correctly, the view you see in the box should look just like the illustration. But the card to the left is actually the card closer to your eye! This is not what your brain will tell you.

Once you've found the correct position for the cut card, tape it in place. You can now show this optical illusion to your friends. Make sure they look in the peephole first, to see the *illusion*, before they look down from the top and see the *reality*.

Fact number 3: Things in the distance look smaller than things close to us. Looking down a busy city street, this certainly seems true. The people close by look "full size," and those far away "look like ants." However, this simple-sounding fact is not always true. The sun appears larger than the moon, for example. Warning: **Do not look directly at the sun.**

According to fact number 3 the sun should be the closer because it is the bigger of the two. But it isn't. The moon is nearly a hundred million miles closer! How does the sun fool us? The sun is almost a million times *larger in diameter* than the moon. Because the sun is so much larger it can be much further away and still appear bigger than the moon. Perhaps you never thought of the sun and moon as an optical illusion, but they are!

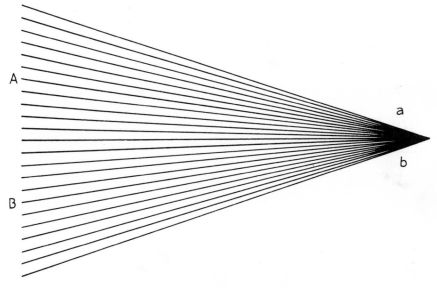

Figure 16

Fact number 3 is called *perspective*, and it is an important principle in art. An artist wishing to draw a picture that will appear accurate, must remember to draw close objects large and distant objects small or an optical illusion will result. Try the following experiment.

Place a paper clip down on either end of the drawing in Figure 16 with one end facing A and the opposite end facing B. Because of the lines, the clip will appear far away if you choose the right side of the drawing to start on or close if you chose the left.

Now, slowly slide the clip sideways along the drawing, keeping it upright, until it reaches the A and B on the opposite side and watch it appear to change its size. Slide the clip back and forth several times. At the "distance" end (right) it

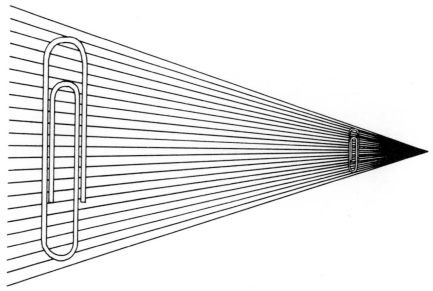

Figure 17

appears enormous because it did not become smaller. That is, an artist drawing this picture who wished to add paper clips would have drawn them smaller at the distant end. The picture would have appeared like Figure 17.

HOW MUCH?

Still another guessing problem we have that sometimes involves an optical illusion is quantity. How much will a container hold? How many beans will fit in a jar?

Years ago storekeepers attracted customers by putting a big sealed jar full of beans in their display window and offering a prize to whoever came closest to guessing the number of beans.

The contest actually was a difficult problem in estimation. Beans are all about the same size so you might not think an optical illusion could be involved, but it could! There was one thing that could change, the *shape of the container* the storekeeper put the beans in (Figure 18).

Of course, because these jars are just flat drawings we can't say how many beans each contains. However, most people would guess there are more beans in a round jar than a tall, skinny one. From our experience, round things just look like more. Yet you know if the tall one were tall enough it certainly could contain the most beans.

Figure 18

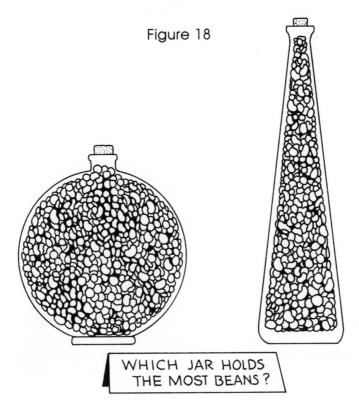

WHICH JAR HOLDS
THE MOST BEANS?

If you are an experimenter, try this: Try to find two differently shaped containers, one round, one tall—like a drinking glass and a vase—that you think will hold the same quantity of water (see Figure 18). When you think you've found the perfect jars, fill one to the top with water, then pour that water into the other container. Does the water reach the exact top of the second container? If it does, you are far better at estimating quantity than most people!

CURVES ARE FOOLERS TOO

Here's one final estimating puzzle for you. Which one of the curves in Figure 19 is the most curved?

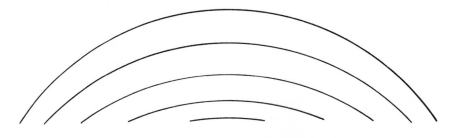

Figure 19

To answer, here's how the curves were drawn: They were all drawn by laying a saucer on paper and drawing part way around the edge! The same saucer was used for each curve. It was simply moved down each time so the curves were drawn under each other, and each curve was drawn shorter than the previous one. If you still can't believe that the curves are all equally curved, find a saucer, pencil, and paper and try it yourself right now!

(32)

We hope you've "learned your lesson" now and will be a more careful guesser on the pages that follow. Optical illusions are fun, but they are also important reminders of why we should use measuring tools like rulers and scales, and not always trust our eyes and brains.

3

EYE DON'T
BELIEVE IT

Close your eyes. Wait. Better read the instructions first.

When your eyes are closed, press the tips of your forefingers against your eyes and rub your eyeballs through your eyelid. Press and rub firmly, *but not hard.* Rub the corners of your eyes especially.

You will "see" tiny spots of light even though your eyes are closed. Try it now.

The lights you see are not really there. They are not the lights in the room, but you are not imagining them either. The lights appear because you are fooling your eyes. To understand what is going on, we must look inside your eye.

A doctor looks inside your eye using an instrument called an ophthalmoscope. This is simply a magnifier and a light which enables the doctor to look through the lens of your eye and see the retina.

The retina of your eye is like the film in a camera. It is sensitive to light. But instead of film, the retina is composed of about 50 million tiny light-sensitive living cells. These cells, called rods and cones, contain an important chemical called visual purple that changes color when light falls on it.

With no light striking the rods and cones, visual purple is a purple color. However, when light enters your eye the visual purple turns yellow. This then sends a signal through your optic nerve to your brain. Your eye in effect says, "I see a light." Your brain then says, "I see the light too." Light, eye, and brain—the three necessities for seeing—working together!

But when you closed your eyes there was no light to cause the visual purple to change color. You caused it to change by rubbing it. When you rubbed your eyeballs you caused the retina to move about a bit also. The rods and cones were stimulated, and some of your visual purple changed to yellow. The message flashed to your brain, and your brain received the signal as, "I see a light." Your eyes gave your brain a faulty message.

The "lights" in the above experiment "flashed" on and off. This is because visual purple changes to yellow for only a fraction of a second, then immediately becomes purple again. Because your finger was moving, the visual purple in one part of your eye gave you only a single "flash." The next "flash" came from another part of your retina.

When your eyes are open and the lights are on, your visual purple is constantly alternating from purple to yellow, to purple, to yellow, telling your brain over and over that your eyes "see light." Your brain "makes sense" of the signals, and forms the tiny messages from the 50 million rods and cones into pictures of your world.

Sometimes visual purple gets overworked and an optical illusion results. If you stare at a light bulb for 15 seconds or so, then look at a wall, you will see a dark spot. The bulb was so bright that your visual purple tired. When you looked away, the part of your retina that worked so hard seeing the bulb now can't see as well as the rest of your retina, so a dark spot results. This illusion is called an afterimage. Fortunately, visual purple refreshes itself quickly, so afterimages don't last long.

A GHOST IN YOUR EYE

Have you ever seen a ghost? You can trick your eyes into seeing one as an afterimage. You will need Figure 20, a bright light, and a blank wall or ceiling.

Have a good bright light shining on this picture of a ghost (we want to tire your retina!). Hold the book about 12 inches (30 centimeters) away from your eyes. Stare at the triangle in the middle of the ghost. Really stare. Don't let your eyes wander off the triangle even if the picture gets blurry and your eyes get tired (that's what we want to happen). Blink if you need to. While you are staring, count *slowly* to 30.

Figure 20

As you are staring and counting, the *white* page of the book glares onto your retina. Your visual purple is changing back and forth and becoming fatigued. But the part of your retina that the image of the black ghost appears on is resting. Objects appear black when light does not reflect off them. The image of the ghost is not affecting the visual purple in that part of your retina.

After reaching "30," shift your eyes to stare at the blank wall or ceiling and hold your eyes still. Continue staring and you should "see" a white ghost appear most mysteriously! The ghost is simply *light* on the wall, except you are seeing the light *brighter* (so it appears white) on the part of your retina that was "resting." That part is in the shape of a ghost!

The nerves from your 50 million rods and cones leave your eye through the optic nerve, which is sort of like a bunch of wires gathered together into a giant cable. The place where the optic nerve leaves your eye enroute to your brain contains no rods or cones, so you cannot see there. This area is known as your blind spot. For fun, we can use it to make a ghost vanish!

As you are looking at Figure 21 an image of the ghost forms on your retinas. Parts of the image are falling on your blind spots (you have two, one in each eye) and you can't see those parts. But because you have two eyes, one eye usually sees the parts of the image falling on the other eye's blind spot, so you are not aware of any missing parts of the image. If, however, you deliberately cause the image of the small ghost to fall completely on one of your blind spots, while you keep the other eye closed, the ghost will vanish.

Here's how. Close your left eye and keep it closed. Now you have only one blind spot in the eye that is open. Stare at the question mark with your right eye only. While staring at the question mark, slowly move this book closer or further away. When the image of the ghost falls on your blind spot, the ghost will vanish! But you must keep looking at the question mark to keep it vanished. If you shift your eye to the right, to see the vanished ghost, its image will move off your blind spot and the ghost will suddenly reappear.

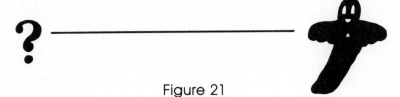

Figure 21

YOUR FABULOUS FOVEA

The fovea, about the size of the head of a pin, is another special spot in your eye. The fovea contains only cone cells and is the part of your eye that sees the sharpest.

Look about the room. Does everything look sharp and clear? That is an optical illusion! The only really sharp parts are those images that fall on your foveas. But because your eyes are always moving, all parts of the room eventually fall on your foveas and your brain remembers them. In your mind, everything seems sharp and clear.

Hard to believe? Here's a quick, simple experiment to prove it.

20

Figure 22

Look directly at the number 20 in Figure 22. When you do, its image falls on your foveas so you see it clearly. It's very sharp, so you can read it easily. But without shifting your eyes, while you stare at the 20, you cannot see what the star design is. You can see "something" on the other side of the page, but it is very blurry.

Now shift your eyes to look at the star and keep your eyes on it. Now you can't read the number 20. In fact, while you stare at the star, if you think about it, all the rest of this page is also out of focus and fuzzy, isn't it? The entire page simply can't all fit on your foveas at the same time.

"QUICKER THAN THE EYE?"

Here is another eye fact that can result in an optical illusion. Your eye has difficulty seeing things that move too quickly. It takes about one-twentieth of a second for visual purple to change to yellow and back to purple. If something moves faster than one-twentieth of a second, your eyes cannot see it well. Of course, your brain steps in and "helps out."

Cut a piece of cardboard about 3 inches by 5 inches (8 centimeters by 13 centimeters). Draw the design shown in Figure 23 and push a pin through the center. Spin the card on the pin while you watch the design. The card will spin faster than one-twentieth of a second so your eye won't be able to "follow" it and the design will become a blur. You will see

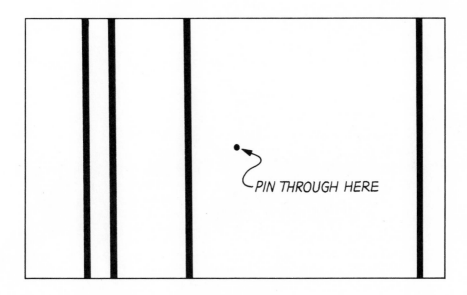

Figure 23

(39)

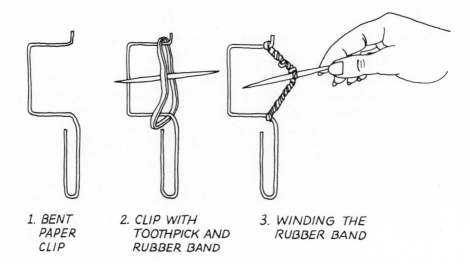

1. BENT
   PAPER
   CLIP

2. CLIP WITH
   TOOTHPICK AND
   RUBBER BAND

3. WINDING THE
   RUBBER BAND

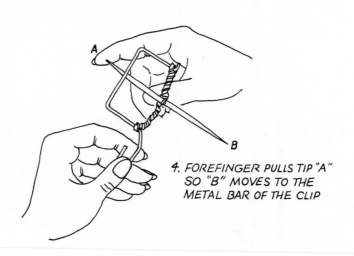

4. FOREFINGER PULLS TIP "A"
   SO "B" MOVES TO THE
   METAL BAR OF THE CLIP

Figure 24

something, however, because your brain will try to make sense out of the blur. If you are like most people, your brain will "see" the straight lines become circles, then, as the spinning card slows down, become lines once again.

Sometimes things move so quickly even your brain can't make sense of it. An optical illusion "magic trick" you can make from a paper clip, rubber band, and toothpick will not only fool your friends but it will fool you too.

Bend the paper clip into the shape shown in Figure 24 and loop a rubber band around it. Slip the toothpick through the band and wind it up tightly. Hold the prepared clip in your left hand and place the tip of your right finger on the end of the toothpick at A and rotate the toothpick until B is underneath the wire.

Let end A slip quickly off your fingertip and the toothpick will appear to snap against the clip and pass right through! You may have to practice a bit to catch on to the fact that what really happens is that the toothpick simply snaps back to its original position. It happens faster than your eye can follow, and your brain "sees" it pass through the metal! A perfect illusion.

A LITTLE COIN-FUSION

Many times optical illusions occur with more than one factor involved. To consider this, here is a closing "magic trick" for you. Please try it before you read the explanation. Try to decide why it fools you. It is an eye illusion, so the reasons have been explained in this chapter.

Hold two coins pinched between your finger and thumb (Figure 25). Slide them back and forth over each other. Keep moving them back and forth, quickly, and you will "see" another coin between them slightly off to the side!

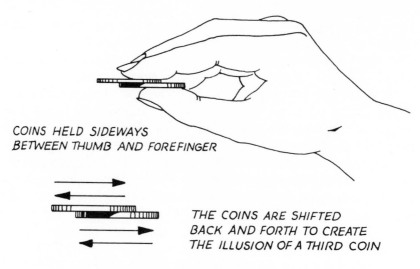

COINS HELD SIDEWAYS
BETWEEN THUMB AND FOREFINGER

THE COINS ARE SHIFTED
BACK AND FORTH TO CREATE
THE ILLUSION OF A THIRD COIN

Figure 25

The illusion is so good you can do it as a trick to cause a coin to "vanish" for a friend. Simply begin by showing the coins to your friend while they are sliding back and forth. Say, "I have three coins, hold out your hand." They look so much like three coins your friend will believe you. Toss them onto your friend's hand saying, "Presto, one coin has vanished!"

The explanation? Have you figured it out? Two eye facts create this illusion.

First, the coins are sliding over one another fast, faster than one-twentieth of a second. Your eye cannot really see them clearly so your brain must "imagine" what's happening. Second, an afterimage is created. Your eyes retain an afterimage of the coins for just a moment, as they did of the ghost. They do this at the end of the slide, where the coins stop, before sliding in the opposite direction. You see a coin in a place where there is no coin, sort of like seeing one coin in two places at the same time.

4

IT'S ALL IN
YOUR HEAD

What does Figure 26 say?

When you first look at it you see two things. You see a sign half covered by a blank rectangle, and you see a word.

Of course, you will agree, there is really no word there. There are some straight and crooked *lines* but no complete letters and no word. But, as you have learned, your eye is only one link in your sight chain. It is not your eye that "sees" the word SCIENCE, it is your *brain*. What your eye sees must be interpreted and understood by your brain.

Figure 26

Sometimes your brain sees more than it should. The science sign is a perfect example. Your eyes see only the top halves of what appear to be some letters. They cannot see the bottom halves because they are not there.

Even if the bottom halves were there your eyes would not see them as letters, only as more lines. It is your brain that recognizes lines as letters, and it has been doing this for you since you first learned to read. In fact, your brain has been doing it so long and so well that now it doesn't even need to see a whole letter, just a part, to see what the letter is. That's what happened when you read the word SCIENCE. Your brain actually saw something that was not there.

Watch it! Your brain does this all the time. It jumps ahead of what your eyes actually see and makes a quick guess. It might have done it this time too. You have no way of telling because you can't actually see under the blank rectangle that covers the bottom halves of the letters. Suppose, however, that blank was a piece of cardboard that got tossed over an old license plate from the imaginary state of OPIL.

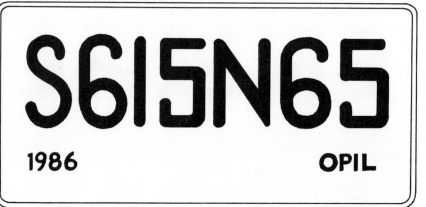

Figure 27

Cover the bottom half of the plate in Figure 27 with a sheet of paper or your hand. The top half of the letters and numbers will look just like the first illustration. Your brain will also see the word SCIENCE, even though you now know it is a number plate that doesn't have a whole word on it.

YOU'RE IMAGINING THINGS

Unlike your eyes, your brain is able to imagine things. "Imagine" is a word that helps explain this type of optical illusion. From past experiences you were able to imagine that the word was SCIENCE from seeing only lines. People imagine, and "see" things that really are not there, all the time.

Many years ago people observed the stars in the sky and, in their minds, grouped bunches of stars together into pictures which today we call constellations. We still see the Big Dipper, Leo The Lion, or Draco The Dragon in the nighttime sky.

Have you ever watched a burning campfire or fireplace and imagined you could see figures and recognizable shapes in it? Or have you "seen" sheep and people and dragons in the clouds? All of these are optical illusions. Your brain is interpeting—making sense of—what your eyes see. Your eyes see stars, fire, and clouds, but your imagination sees other things it recognizes.

QUICKNESS OF THE BRAIN

Your brain has a remarkable ability to make sense out of everything it sees, even things that are new, different, or just part of something. Your brain probably does it thousands of times every day. In fact, often your brain doesn't even take time to see a "whole" before it sees something.

For example,

WHEN YOU CAREFULLY READ THE
THE WORDS IN A PARAGRAPH LIKE
LIKE THIS ONE IT IS EASY TO
TO MAKE A MISTAKE. IN
IN FACT YOU MIGHT BE
BE MAKING ONE RIGHT NOW
NOW UNLESS YOU ARE
ARE READING VERY, VERY SLOWLY!

Probably it just happened to you! As we read, scientists say, we see words in groups and form a picture in our minds of what each group of words is saying. People who read very quickly do this better than slow readers. They can see larger groups of words in a single glance.

If you are a fast reader you probably didn't even notice that, in the paragraph above, the last word in every line was also the first word in the following line. Your eyes flicked over them so quickly, you read in groups of words, not by individual words. Even if you finally caught on, it probably took your brain several sentences to catch the trick wording.

Psychologists use a Rorschach test (named after the man who developed it) to study how an individual's mind thinks. The Rorschach test is simply a series of ink blots originally made by spilling liquid ink on a paper, then folding the paper in two to produce a double blot with each side being a mirror image of the other. Because many things in our world are right-and-left sided these ink blots remind us of objects and living things.

When we take the test, the psychologist asks us to describe what we "see" (imagine) in the ink blot. Comparing our descriptions with those from many others tells the psychologist about our personalities, and our ways of looking at the world, as compared to other people's.

Figure 28

The ink blot in Figure 28 is not from the Rorschach test, but you will still easily be able to imagine it as something. Perhaps you can even create a mini-story about what's going on in it. What do you see? You might find it an interesting project to make other ink blots yourself and ask your friends what they see in them. Do they imagine the same things you do? Remember, though, that it takes many thousands of tests, plus a trained psychologist to really interpret ink blot tests.

IT'S IN YOUR MIND

There are other ways our brains fool us into seeing things as they are not. In Chapter 3 you learned that the eye contains a blind spot and, experimenting with it, you were able to make a ghost vanish simply by having its image fall there. This illusion was created by your eye's lack of vision cells in one spot. If you try a similar experiment, but allow the brain to take part, quite a different result occurs.

(47)

Close your left eye and keep it closed. Look at the X beside the black bars in Figure 29. While keeping your eye fixed on the X, move the book closer and further from your eye. At one point the BLANK SPACE between the long and short black bars will fall on your blind spot. When it does, of course, your *eye* will not see the blank space. However, your *brain* will immediately recognize this fact and make up for it by creating a picture for you of one continuous black bar with no break in it at all!

Figure 29

Here your eye and brain were not a dependable team. Your eye sent a true message that the bar had a place that it could not see, but your brain saw a continuous long black bar. Rather than a "blind spot," this was a filled-in "mind spot!"

RIGHT IN FRONT
OF YOUR NOSE

Do you know that there is a place right before your eyes where you cannot see? Try this: Hold your index finger pointing up in front of your eyes about 6 inches (15 centimeters) from the bridge of your nose. Slowly move the fingertip toward your nose, right between your eyes, while you watch it (it will get blurry and look like two fingers), until it is about a half-inch (1 to 2 centimeters) from your nose. When it almost touches the bridge of your nose, the tip of the finger vanishes.

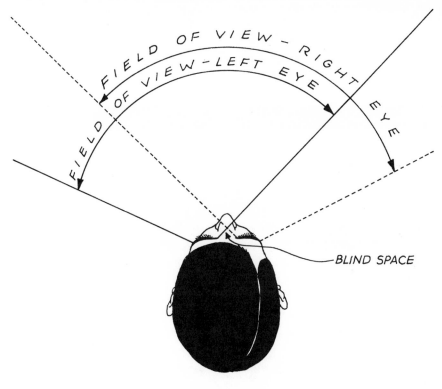

Figure 30

You have two eyes, and each has a *field of view.* The field of view from one eye overlaps the other so we have a wide field, as Figure 30 shows. But you will notice that the field of view of both eyes misses that space just in front of the bridge of your nose. When your fingertip moved there, it simply went out of your field of view and it couldn't be seen any more than if you had placed it behind your head, which is also out of your field of view. Sometimes this blind space can give your brain a problem. Suppose your brain encounters a picture, part of which is in your field of view and part of which is out. Figure 31 shows such a picture.

You must put the image of the space between the two black bars out of your field of view while leaving the bars themselves in.

Figure 31

To accomplish this, move the book very close to your eyes, watching the black bars, until the blank space between them is just touching the bridge of your nose. When the blank space goes out of your field of view your brain compensates by simply *ignoring it.* Your eyes see only the bars, so your brain "joins them together" to make one continuous bar just as it did when it couldn't "see" the blank space in the previous blind spot experiment.

TWO EYES . . . TOO WISE?

The fact that you have two eyes—each making a separate picture—means extra work for your brain. Your brain has the task of blending the two pictures together to create a single picture of what the eyes see. Usually your brain does this perfectly, even giving you the ability to see *depth* or in three dimensions (if you close one eye you lose this). Your brain does this continuously, and usually (except for optical illusions) without error.

But what if each eye sees something different? Your brain will always attempt to blend the two pictures to make a sensible single picture. Try looking at Figure 32 from reading distance. Both eyes see the same image—the top of a rabbit

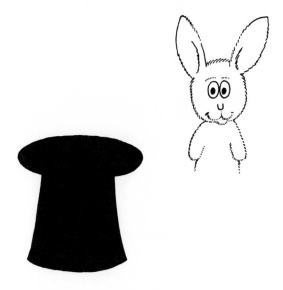

Figure 32

beside a magician's hat. This interpretation by your brain of what you are seeing is absolutely correct.

Now confuse your brain. Move the book slowly toward your eyes until the tip of your nose touches the page *between* the rabbit and the hat. When the book touches your nose, the image of the rabbit alone will be in your right eye and the image of the hat in your left. Your brain, confused, will blend the pictures together and give you a single, false, picture of the rabbit sitting in the magician's hat!

You can use this same principle to "create motion" using one still picture. Hold this book so that Figure 33 is against your face and the juggler's head touches the tip of your nose. The images of some of the balls are in your right eye, and others are in your left. If you now twist the book quickly

Figure 33

back and forth the balls will be going up in one eye and down in the other. With a bit of experimenting you should be able to convince your brain that the single picture it creates is that of balls moving in different directions!

We can't say that all optical illusions are in your mind, but we certainly can say that *many* of them are!

5

COLORS
CAN
CONFUSE

The square in Figure 34 contains an optical illusion!

Don't be fooled into thinking there is nothing in the square for your eyes to see. It's true there is no picture, but there *is* white light. Your eyes can see the color white, so you see a white square. You will learn in this chapter that "white" is just a wonderful optical illusion!

Figure 34

Our eyes see more than just pictures, they see color. Most animals do not share this ability which we take for granted. When a bullfighter waves a red cape before a bull, the bright red color pleases the eyes of the audience, not the bull, for

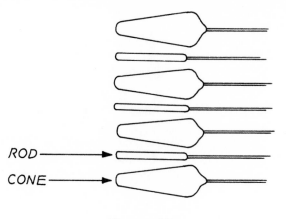

Figure 35

bulls are colorblind and see the cape only as dark gray. (It is the movement of the cape, not its color, that excites the bull.)

How does a scientist know that bulls are colorblind?

The eye's retina, you may recall, is made of about 50 million tiny light-sensitive cells called rods and cones (Figure 35). These cells hold the mystery of color vision.

Rod cells are sensitive to tiny amounts of light. They enable us to see in dark conditions. We enter a movie theater while the show is in progress, and at first we cannot see at all. Then our eyes "become accustomed to the dark" and we can see our way to a seat. But we do not see the seat in color! Rod cells cannot see color.

Cone cells cannot "see" unless there is plenty of light. They cannot function and are essentially "blind" in the dark movie theater. When there is plenty of light, however, cone cells see sharply and in color. (The fovea, where you see sharpest, is made only of cone cells.)

It is not known exactly how cone cells see color, but we do know color "happens" within them. To decide whether an animal can see color, therefore, a scientist examines a retina from its eye under a powerful microscope. If cone cells are found, the animal is assumed to see color; if none are found the animal is colorblind.

Of course, people can also be colorblind, even though they have cone cells. Colorblindness is more common in male humans; females carry the genes for colorblindness, but are rarely colorblind themselves. That means if you are colorblind, you probably inherited the trait from your mother, who most likely has normal color vision. At present there is no remedy for colorblindness.

INSTANT COLORBLINDNESS

What's it like to be colorblind? That is hard for someone who is not colorblind to imagine. If you were totally colorblind the world would appear only in black, white, and shades of gray. To experience this, simply watch a program on a black-and-white television set or look at black-and-white photos in the newspaper. That's the way a totally colorblind person sees everything.

Fortunately, most colorblind people aren't totally color-blind. Most have a color *confusion,* which simply means they see colors differently from color-correct people. Hold a piece of transparent colored plastic before your eyes and the world will appear only in black and the color of the plastic. This is the way a color-confused person might see things.

Even people who see color correctly can be easily fooled by it. For example, if you said the square at the start of this chapter was white you may be wrong.

Try this: find a separate piece of white paper and lay it so it overlaps the square in this book. Do they both appear to be the same color? Probably not! One probably seems to be a bit grayer by comparison. Even white comes in different

Figure 36

shades. Usually we are not aware of this fact. This is an effect of *contrast.* The exact color seen depends greatly on what other colors are around it. Here is an experiment that will show this effect.

The red bar in Figure 36 is surrounded by yellow on one side and black on the other. Place your finger over the red bar right in the middle where the yellow and black meet. This hides the fact that the red bar is a continuous one of the same shade of red (which it is) and creates a "block" of red to contrast with the blocks of yellow and black. The red blocks no longer appear to be the same shade of red. You must remove your finger to convince yourself that they are.

Most people are concerned about wearing clothes with pleasing color combinations. Some people feel that red and orange, for example, are colors that "clash" so badly they would never consider wearing them together. Other people wouldn't be caught dead wearing brown socks and blue jeans.

"Clash" is an expression we use when colors contrast in a manner that is not pleasing to us. We would all agree that red, orange, brown, and blue are wonderful colors, and we would miss them if they vanished. But if the contrast is too great they can clash. Clashing is actually an optical illusion!

Figure 37

Sometimes colors contrast with one another so dramatically that our eyes and brains have great difficulty adjusting to them. Watch the red blob in Figure 37 as you gently shake and twist the book back and forth. The blob appears to wiggle and rock as though it were made of gelatin.

One explanation is that our eyes retain the image of a warm color (red) a bit longer than a cold color (green). Although both colors move sidewise together when you move the book, the red image tends to linger a bit behind. Your brain then sees the red moving differently from the green.

ALL THE COLORS
IN THE RAINBOW

This chapter began by saying that white is an optical illusion. Over three hundred years ago the scientist Sir Isaac Newton discovered this fact. When Sir Issac placed a triangular block of glass called a prism in a beam of white sunlight, bands of different colors emerged from the prism.

White is not a color. It is made of a mixture of colors, called the *spectrum:* red, orange, yellow, green, blue, and violet. When these colors are blended together, our eye can't detect the individual colors and our brain calls what we do see white.

In this respect your ear is better than your eye. If you listen to a band playing, you enjoy the music made from many different instruments. If you wish, however, you can tune in just one of the instruments, say, the flute, and you will hear that one instrument clearly and distinctly.

But look at the white block at the beginning of this chapter. You now know that it is not a white block, but is actually a block containing every color of the spectrum. Try to see just the color red in that block! As hard as you try, your eye won't be able to pick out red or any other individual color from the white block the way your ear is able to pick out the flute from the band music.

When sunlight passes through tiny water droplets in the sky, we sometimes see a rainbow. This again demonstrates

Figure 38

that white light is a mixture of colors. Figure 38 shows a color drawing of a rainbow. How many colors is it created from?

If you said six you are wrong. *Real* rainbows have six major colors. However this is not a real rainbow. It is a drawing of one!

Colored pictures in books and magazines are yet another type of optical illusion. They are made by printing only three colors plus black, and the white of the paper. The picture of the rainbow above was run through the press four times. Each time one of the colors or black was printed on top of the previous one. Figure 39 shows the rainbow printed in the colors used for each printing.

Figure 40 shows how the picture "developed" as each color was added.

You do not "see" all the colors of the rainbow until the last ink is added. Then suddenly you see all the colors in the

MAGENTA

CYAN

YELLOW

BLACK

Figure 39

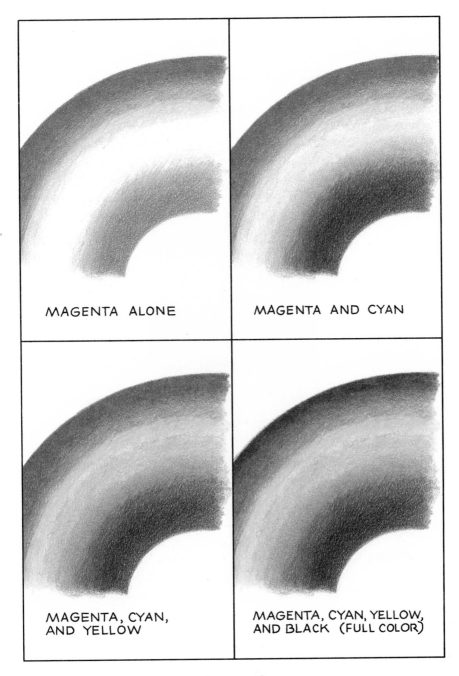

MAGENTA ALONE

MAGENTA AND CYAN

MAGENTA, CYAN,
AND YELLOW

MAGENTA, CYAN, YELLOW,
AND BLACK (FULL COLOR)

Figure 40

spectrum, even though they were not used in the printing process. Scientists don't know what happens in our eyes and brain that creates a full-color image from just three colors of ink (plus black).

Perhaps one of the most surprising color optical illusions is a colored afterimage. Not only can the retina of your eye "see" a picture after looking away from the actual picture, but it can do it in color! Figure 41 shows a playing card. The card is familiar, but the color is wrong. Its afterimage will surprise you.

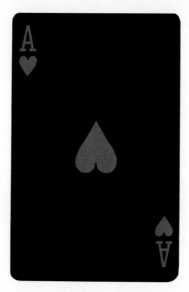

Figure 41

Hold the card in bright light and stare at the center of the heart. Count slowly to 30 without shifting your eyes (it's okay to blink). Then shift your eyes to the ceiling or a blank wall and stare at the wall or ceiling. A playing card will appear on the ceiling or wall as an afterimage. Amazingly it will be a *white* card with *red* hearts!

Because the blank wall has white light reflecting from its surface, all of the colors are there also. As you stared at the green hearts, your cone cells tired of this color. When you shifted your vision to the ceiling your eyes did not respond strongly to the green color in the white light. Rather they responded strongly to the opposite color to green, which is red. For the first time perhaps, you *were* able to separate a single color from white light, but only for a few moments, and only by tricking your eyes into doing it.

Interestingly, you will *always* see the opposite color as an afterimage (even white as the opposite of black). You can even use this fact to discover opposite colors without knowing what they are beforehand.

Simply stare at a brightly lighted square of any color you are curious about, then look at a blank wall and you will see an afterimage square of its opposite color. If you stare at a red ace of hearts from an ordinary deck of cards you will see a black and green afterimage as shown above. You can even see several different opposite colors at the same time. A classic optical illusion is to stare at a flag, from any country, then look at a blank wall to see the same flag in its opposite colors.

A COLOR-CHANGING CRITTER

Because color afterimages are so interesting, let's close this chapter with a "laboratory" of experiments you can try. For fun, we'll call it The Strange Beast With The Color-Changing Spots.

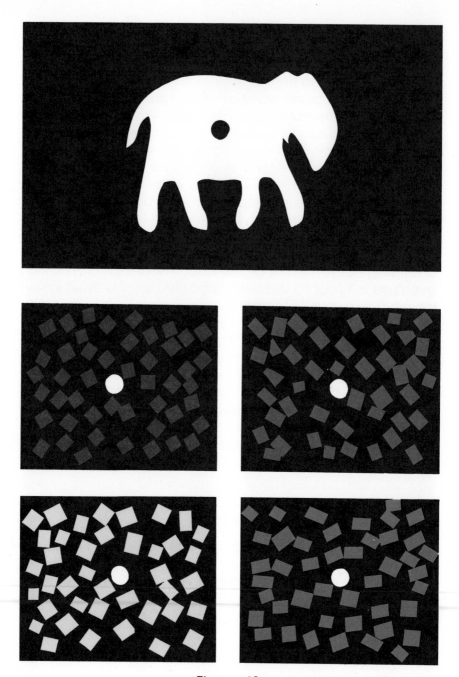

Figure 42

Simply stare at the dot in the center of any of the spots blocks in Figure 42 (one at a time) and count to 30. Then shift your gaze to stare at the spot in the center of the beast. Continue staring and in a moment, spots will appear to cover it and, of course, they will be the opposite color of the spot you stared at.

6

OP-TRICKS
AROUND US

Have you ever seen a picture like the one in Figure 43? There is a good chance you see a picture something like this one regularly. It is a picture of a bicycle, but the picture is distorted, and for a very good reason.

Try this: Tip the top of this book *away* from your eyes so you are looking along the page. The page should be held quite flat, like a tabletop, with your eyes looking at it from the edge.

As you look at the page and tip the book you will discover that the picture no longer appears distorted. The bicycle straightens out and appears to be drawn correctly.

This picture is drawn from the bicycle design that is painted on the pavement of roads near schools and other places where children might be riding bikes. The drawing warns an automobile driver of this and cautions him to be alert. Because the driver sees the road *from an angle*, the drawing must be distorted to appear correct.

Now draw a bicycle similar to the one shown, on a scrap of paper, but do not make your drawing distorted. Next, view your drawing from the edge as you tip the top away from your eyes, and you will see a very distorted bicycle. This is just what the automobile driver would see if the warning sign had been painted to look like a real bicycle.

Figure 43

If you look at almost any of the giant words that highway crews paint on the street—STOP, CAUTION, SLOW—you will discover that they too are distorted when you look straight down on them. The words are done in long, skinny writing so the letters will appear the correct size and shape when viewed at an angle out of the windshield of an automobile.

You can quickly learn to write secret messages in long skinny writing. Figure 44 shows a card created by a magician named Orville Meyer. Find his name and see how he did it. Then try writing *your* name in long, skinny writing the same way.

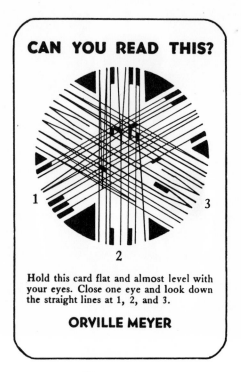

CAN YOU READ THIS?

1

2

3

Hold this card flat and almost level with your eyes. Close one eye and look down the straight lines at 1, 2, and 3.

ORVILLE MEYER

Figure 44

KEEP YOUR EYES OPEN!

Optical illusions are all around us. Some people even use them to change their appearance. People who are embarrassed because they are too thin learn to wear bright-colored clothes and clothing with stripes that run sideways because it makes them appear larger. People who think they are too fat discover that wearing darker clothes and stripes that run up and down make them appear thinner. Of course thin people don't really get fatter nor do fat people really get thinner; they are making optical illusions work for them. Look for yourself the next time you see a lot of people.

You can also study optical illusions the next time you are in a grocery store. Observe the cans and packages as you consider this one simple optical illusion fact: *dark colored objects appear smaller than light colored objects.* If two identical boxes of breakfast cereal are side by side, but one is brilliant yellow with bright red lettering and the other is deep purple with dark green lettering, the yellow box will always look larger.

Remembering this as you study the grocery store products you will discover that practically all of the products offered for sale are in light and brightly colored packages and cans. In fact, you probably won't be able to find anything in a box or can "deep purple with dark green lettering"! Not only have manufacturers learned that people like bright colors and are attracted to them, but they also know that bright colors convince people they are getting more for their money.

LOOK IN ANY BOOK

The book you are reading is filled with optical illusions. No, not just the illustrations but the kind of optical illusions you will find in any book if you know where, and how, to look for them.

The famous illusion shown in Figure 45 is known to all printers. It has to do with the way our eyes and brain "see" the printed number "8" and the capital letter "S." Study the lines of 8's and S's. Do you notice that the bottom section of each appears to be smaller than the top section? That is the way they really are in a printed book, except we have deliberately printed them upside down so you can see it. Turn the book upside down and look at the lines of 8's and S's again. They will appear correctly shaped with both top and bottom the same size. They aren't the same; it's simply an unusual optical illusion trick that printers learned many years ago.

88888
SSSSS

Figure 45

No one knows exactly why we view these characters in this manner, but the amazing fact is that almost every book uses lopsided 8's and S's just so the reader won't "see" them looking lopsided!

Flip through this book right now and find a capital "S" or an "8" and turn the book over to view it upside down. You'll find it is lopsided too! And, while you are searching, check out a capital "B" (how about this one). Is it lopsided too?

Magazines and newspapers are filled with photos that are optical illusions. Study a newspaper photograph through a magnifying glass and you will discover it is made of thousands of tiny dots of ink. If it is a colored picture in a magazine you will find it too is made of tiny dots and each dot is a special color. Without the magnifying glass, however, your eyes have difficulty seeing the individual dots, so your brain is able to blend the thousands of separate points into a single "picture."

This, in effect, reflects the ability of your brain to make "wholes" out of individual parts. Your brain prefers not to see dots but to make sense out of them. If it were not for this wonderful ability, imagine how confusing a newspaper or magazine picture would be.

Figure 46 shows what a part of a newspaper photo would look like through a powerful magnifying glass. We have enlarged a part of the picture so the dots will appear obvious

Figure 46

to your eye. Your brain also "sees" the dots and it has great difficulty trying to form a single picture from them. But try this: Prop this book upright on a desk so you can see the dots. Back away from the book slowly. As you move further away, the dots will appear to get smaller until they finally will be small enough for your brain to ignore them separately and form a single picture.

NATURE HAS THEM TOO

Nature too is filled with optical illusions. If you look along a long stretch of blacktop highway on a very hot day you may see "puddles of water" which do not actually exist.

These are caused by the hot tar heating a thin layer of air directly above it, which causes a bending of the light passing through that air. This causes the heated air to appear different to your eye from the cooler air just above it. This strange sight, called a *mirage* (Figure 47), can also happen in the middle of a dry desert, luring thirsty travelers to a "pond" that is not really there.

Figure 47 Mirage in the Sahara Desert in North Africa

Figure 48
Can you find
the pipefish?

Many animals are colored in a pattern which matches their surroundings. This is called *camouflage.* A tiger resting in a field of tall reeds is practically impossible to see. The tiger's orange color and thin vertical stripes match the color and appearance of the field perfectly. An owl, with drab, gray-streaked feathers and "ear tufts" on its head, vanishes when it rests on a dead tree limb. The owl's color duplicates the tree's bark, and the ear tufts cause it to resemble a branch that has broken off at the top.

Still other animals can change their color to match their surroundings. A squid, in the ocean, becomes light tan color while swimming over a sandy bottom, then instantly turns almost black when it swims over dark seaweed! The pipefish in Figure 48 is well camouflaged against the turtle grass.

(73)

Are you a moonwatcher? If so, you are already familiar with one of nature's greatest optical illusions. The moon itself seems to change its size depending on where you see it.

If you observe the moon just as it is rising, it appears extremely large. Later, when it is high in the sky, it appears considerably smaller. Scientists investigating this optical illusion have discovered that some people have thought the moon was up to thirty times bigger upon its first rising than later.

Why does this occur? Of course the moon doesn't change its size one bit, but it does change its position. When it is close to the horizon we see it along with other objects on the horizon, objects we are familiar with: trees, buildings, and so on.

Our brain instantly compares the size of the moon with the size of these familiar things. Later, when the moon is far above them, we again make the comparison. But now the moon appears much further away so our brain perceives it as smaller. See for yourself the next time the moon is full and the sky is clear.

MOVING PICTURES
DON'T REALLY MOVE

Perhaps one of the most common and important optical illusions you encounter regularly are the "moving pictures" in television and motion pictures.

In fact, neither television nor motion pictures really move, and that is the illusion. A "show" is composed of hundreds of thousands of individual "still" pictures flashed one after another on the screen. Each separate picture is just slightly different from the one before, and your brain is able to "see" the difference as movement. Your eyes and brain are both

Figure 49

involved. If either worked differently from the way it does there would be no such thing as television or motion pictures in your world.

The best way to understand how television or motion pictures appear to move is to actually make a simple two-picture movie yourself.

Several things are required. You must have two identical pictures with a *slight* difference in position (which will be the movement), you must allow your eyes to see each picture one at a time, and the change from one picture to the other must be done quickly, in less than 1/20 of a second.

Cut a strip of paper about 11 inches (28 centimeters) long and 3 inches (8 centimeters) wide. Fold it in half across the center. Following Figure 49 trace the figure on the lower half of the paper strip. Next fold the paper in half and hold it up to a window so you can see the traced figure through the top sheet of paper. Trace the figure again, but this time change the position of the head, arms, and legs as suggested in the drawing.

To change from one drawing to another quickly and automatically, roll the top sheet tightly around a pencil. Then remove the pencil. The paper will remain rolled. Holding the paper down on a table, flick the rolled-up sheet with the eraser end of the pencil to unroll the top sheet so its picture covers the lower one for a moment. Immediately move the pencil back so the sheet rolls up once again to show the lower picture. By flicking the pencil back and forth rapidly you will see first one picture then the other. The little figure will appear to move.

What is happening here is exactly what happens, using many thousands of pictures, on television and in motion pictures. Your eye has the ability to retain an image for a short time after it is gone. Your eye can retain the image of one figure while the pencil flicks the next one into position. It then sees the next one as a continuation of the first. Your brain interprets this "continuation" as movement because parts of the picture are now in different positions.

If you slowly pull a length of movie film through your hands you can easily see the individual frames. You see no motion. The separate pictures are moving too slowly to trick your eyes and to puzzle your brain into creating the illusion of motion.

EVEN IN YOUR POCKET

You can find a final everyday optical illusion right in your wallet if you have a dollar bill. The portrait of George Washington has been drawn in a special way. It is a technique that portrait painters discovered many years ago. Once you know the trick you can see it in many paintings of people's faces.

Look directly into George's eyes. In fact, stare into them. You will notice that he is looking directly toward you. Now turn the bill slightly to one side so the portrait is turned to the side. George will still be looking directly at you! Slowly twist the bill back and forth. No matter how you turn the picture, George will always be looking directly into your eyes. You may even swear his eyes are turning toward you.

Why does this happen? The technique, discovered by some long-ago portrait painter, was to combine two different views of a person to make one. If you cover Washington's eyes you will discover that the artist has drawn his head facing to one side. Next cover Washington's head, as best you can, so only the eyes show and you will discover the secret. The eyes have been drawn looking straight ahead as they would be drawn in a head-on portrait! The angle of the eyes actually does not go with the angle of the head, but it appears to.

Your brain tells you George is facing to the side, while his eyes stare straight at you. No matter how you turn the picture his eyes will continue to stare at you, straight on, reminding you that optical illusions are everywhere. You only have to look for them!

7

IT'S A
MAGICIAN'S
JOB

"Pick a card, any card . . ."

   Figure 50 shows two that we've already picked for you. Please remember your cards so we can do a magic trick with them later in this chapter.

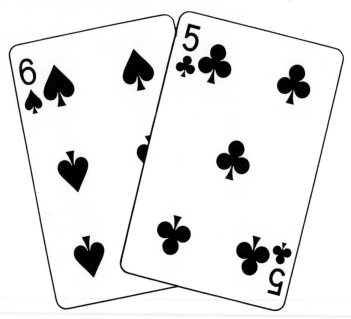

Figure 50

Do you enjoy magic tricks? When a magician pulls a rabbit from an "empty" hat most people are puzzled and fasci-
nated. If you try to figure out how the trick works, you're even
more puzzled. The harder you look, the more the magician
seems to fool you. You say, "I see it, but I don't believe it!"
That's the same thing we say when we see an optical illusion!
"I see it but I don't believe it!"

Many—in fact most—magic tricks are optical illusions,
tricks that fool our eyes and our brain. The title of this chapter
tells you this. It's a magician's job to USE optical illusions to
cause you to see the wrong things at the right times. A rabbit
couldn't really appear in an empty hat. It must have either
been in there all along but hidden in some way so your eyes
couldn't see it, or the magician must have fooled your eyes
into looking somewhere else at the moment he or she
secretly put the rabbit into the hat.

Either way, the magician tricked your eyes and your brain
and created an optical illusion which you could only interpret
as "pulling a rabbit out of an empty hat."

Magicians use many of the ideas we have investigated in
this book. Now that you have studied these ideas too, perhaps you would like to put them to use by becoming a magician and fooling your friends.

THE SHRUNKEN DOLLAR BILL

Take an ordinary dollar bill and accordian pleat it first one
way, then the other way. Make the pleats as small as you
possibly can—the more, the better. Refer to Figure 51.

Open the bill out flat and then gather it into a ball by
wadding in from the ends. When it is formed into a ball, roll
the ball hard between the palms of your hands. Again, the
tighter you do this the better the effect will be.

Finally, open the bill and smooth it out. When you first see
it even you will be surprised. The bill appears to be consider-

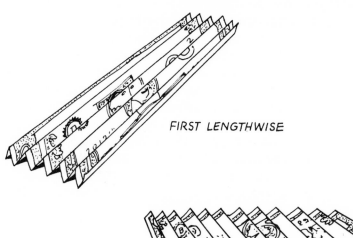

FIRST LENGTHWISE

THEN SIDEWAYS

FINALLY, ROLL INTO A TIGHT BALL

Figure 51

ably smaller than it should be! It appears as a perfect dollar bill but tiny.

Of course, it's an optical illusion. The many tiny creases simply make the bill appear smaller. It is your brain that is surprised. The bill looks wrong only because you are so familiar with the actual size of a dollar bill, which we usually see in a flat condition.

You can carry this tiny bill in your wallet if you wish and take it out to show your friends how "little money" you have. Or tell them you use it to make "small purchases." Or you can use it to show another optical illusion by causing it to grow back to its original size.

To accomplish this, simply hold it by both ends and slowly, firmly, draw it back and forth over the edge of a table. This will flatten out the tiny creases. "Magically" the bill will appear to grow larger as you watch!

This is a trick of *estimation*, and as you learned in previous chapters, your eyes and brain can't be trusted to guess sizes of things. The following trick also works because of this.

THE CURVED-STICKS
ILLUSION

You can use one of the best-known optical illusions as a magic trick. It's a perfect trick to do at a party because it can be seen by everyone and it makes people laugh. The illusion is known as the curved-sticks illusion and you have probably seen it before because it has appeared in many books. Usually it appears simply as a picture, like Figure 52.

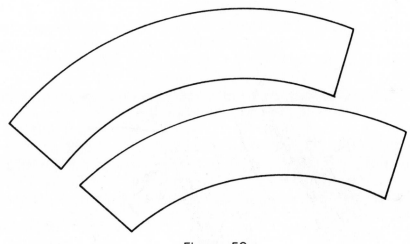

Figure 52

Which curved stick is longer? Most people know that even though the bottom one *looks* longer, they are exactly the same size. To use this as a magic trick, you must present the illusion differently.

Draw one curved stick on a sheet of heavy paper or cardboard. Make it as large as you like—the larger the better, particularly if you wish to show it to several people or an audience. When you have drawn it, carefully cut it out with a pair of scissors. Next lay this curved stick on another sheet of paper and trace around it to create a second, duplicate stick, except make this second stick a little longer than the first one. Cut this stick out also. You are now ready to present the trick. You need only the two curved sticks and the scissors.

Hand your friend the scissors and ask her to help you for a minute. Show her the two curved sticks, holding them separated, one in each hand. Explain that you are trying to cut these two curves to be the same length but one always seems to be longer than the other.

Your friend may be familiar with the optical illusion and suspect a trick but you immediately lay one stick on top of the other (don't hold them one above the other, as in the illustration; they should be held together like the slices of bread in a sandwich at this point) and line up the ends. Your friend will now see one is definitely longer than the other.

Immediately remove the longer one and ask your friend to trim a piece off the end so it will be the same length as the other. She does. Now they probably really are about the same length. But, when you hold them up to check, hold the one just cut under the other so they appear as in the illustration. The bottom one, just cut, will appear much shorter than the top one! Tell your friend that she cut off too much and offer the top stick for her to trim a bit off. Then, to check, hold that one *under* the other and once again it appears that she trimmed too much.

At this point the sticks are really different lengths, so you can "help" your assistant by laying the sticks one on top of the other and letting her snip off both ends at the same time (like trimming the crust off a sandwich) so the sticks "must be the same size." But then, because this is an optical illusion, when you hold one above the other the lower one will still look shorter.

Continue this trimming and exchanging places until your friend has trimmed both sticks entirely away. Then tell her, "That's the last time I'll ever ask you to do a simple job for me."

THE KARATE CHOP
CARD TRICK

Every magician should know a card trick. Most magicians know dozens. Some require clever sleight-of-hand, but the following card trick uses only "sleight-of-brain!"

DON'T TURN BACK ANY PAGES! Read the entire paragraph below.

This chapter began by showing you two playing cards and asking you to remember them. Just for fun, without turning back, see if you can pick out your two cards from the pairs of cards shown in Figure 53.

If you have a good memory and you are a good observer, you probably did not have any difficulty recalling and finding your cards. The challenge seems so simple. But do not forget that this is a book about optical illusions. There may be a trick here. If you think your cards were the six of clubs and the 5 of spades, turn back to the beginning of the chapter and look carefully.

Figure 53

Rather than looking carefully and separately at the exact values of the cards you saw them as a single unit. Your brain saw a club, a spade, a six, and a five, but it saw them "together" and it was this picture that you remembered. In Figure 53 your brain saw the same values and recognized the clubs and spades and the five and six as the same picture you saw at the chapter opening.

By using real cards and a story you can present this optical illusion as a magic trick.

Secretly arrange four cards in a deck. Place the 5 of spades on the bottom of the deck and the 6 of clubs on top of the deck. Next place the 6 of spades and the 5 of clubs on top of the deck (on the 6 of clubs). Do this carefully so you won't be confused. Save the confusion for your *audience*, which won't know about this secret preparation.

Tell your audience that you will show them your famous Karate Chop Card Trick. Remove the two top cards (6 of spades and 5 of clubs) and show them—hold them together but fanned out so the audience sees both cards. *Do not call them by name.* Just show them as you say, "I will use these two cards, which I will place in the middle of the deck."

Ask a spectator to cut the deck somewhere near the middle. Drop one of your cards face down on the cut deck and ask the person to drop the top portion of the deck on it. Ask that the deck be cut again and add the other card. Explain that the cards are now completely lost somewhere in the center of the deck and you will attempt to find them using only karate!

Give the deck a hard karate chop.

Flip the deck over so the bottom card (5 of spades) shows. Remove it, saying, "There's the first one." Immediately give the face up deck another hard karate chop and flip it over, face down. Remove the top card (6 of clubs) and toss it, face up, beside the 5 of spades as you say, "And there's the other one!"

Not one person in one hundred will recognize that the two cards now laying on the table are NOT the same two cards you inserted into the center of the deck. Try it and see how easy it is to fool people with an "op-trick" illusion!

This chapter did not teach you how to pull rabbits from hats or make elephants vanish. This is not a magic book. It is a book about optical illusions. Magic is included because many magic tricks are optical illusions. If you enjoyed this chapter's sample of "how to be a magician" you can find entire books on the subject at the library. As you read them, remember that they are optical illusion books too. As you try the tricks it might be fun to consider how they fool people— brains? eyes? light? Think of the ideas you have read about in the previous pages, cells in your retina, blind spots, perspective, afterimages, color confusions, and the many more things involved in "seeing." You will discover them all in the magician's bag of tricks.

Perhaps *this* book is a magic book after all.

BIBLIOGRAPHY

Armstrong, Tim. *The Moving Pattern Book: How to Make Optical Illusions of Your Own*. Los Angeles: Price, Stern, Sloan, 1983.

Beeler, Nelson F., and Franklyn Branley. *Experiments in Optical Illusion*. New York: Crowell, 1951.

Cole, K. C. *Facets of Light: Colors, Images, and Things That Glow in the Dark*. San Francisco: Exploratorium, 1980.

_____. *Vision: In the Eye of the Beholder*. San Francisco: Exploratorium, 1978.

Gregory, R. L., and E. H. Gombrich, eds. *Illusion in Nature and Art*. New York: Scribner's, 1974.

Kettlekamp, Larry. *Tricks of Eye and Mind: The Story of Optical Illusion*. New York: Morrow, 1974.

Lanners, Edi. *Illusions*. Translated and adapted by Heinz Norden. New York: Holt, Rinehart & Winston, 1977.

Luckiesh, M. *Visual Illusions: Their Causes, Characteristics and Applications*. New York: Dover, 1965.

Newell, Peter. *Topsys & Turvys*. New York: Dover, 1964.

INDEX

ABOUT
THE
AUTHORS

Laurence B. White is director of an elementary school science center and has written numerous children's books, including *Science Games, Science Tricks*, and *Science Toys*. Ray Broekel has written over one hundred children's books, many textbooks, and two adult books on chocolate. Laurence and Ray have written several children's books together, but *Optical Illusions* is their first for Franklin Watts.